Gabriel Massias

Stock Market Investing for Beginners

Everything You Need to Start Making Money Today

The 3M Bros Company

I would like to express my gratitude to my uncle Roland, who has always been a mentor and guide to me. His support and advice were invaluable during the writing of this book.

I'm proud to be able to share this knowledge with you, and I'm convinced that the information presented will help you take control of your financial future.

Thanks again, Roland, for your contribution to my development!

« Rule n°1 is never to lose money.

Rule n°2 is to never forget rule n°1. »

Warren Buffett

« It's always the impatience to win that makes you lose. »

Louis XIV

« Compound interest is the eighth wonder of the world.

He who understands it, gets rich; he who doesn't, pays for it. »

Albert Einstein

Contents

Why do you need this book?

Investing in the stock market seems intimidating, especially when you don't know all the ins and outs of the system. But have you ever imagined what your life could be like if you had access to extra money to make your dreams come true?

If you're ready to step out of your comfort zone and invest in your future, then this is the book for you!

It all started when I was young. Back then, I firmly believed that to be financially successful, you simply had to work hard and save money. However, as I grew older, I realized that this strategy wouldn't allow me to achieve the financial results I really wanted.

I discovered this exciting world at a family dinner, where my maternal uncle, Roland, shared his knowledge with me. Roland was a successful businessman, and I was very inspired by his financial success.

He told me how he managed to accumulate so much wealth. He explained that he started investing as soon as he had his first income. He showed me how he invested in stocks, ETFs and real estate to make his money grow over the long term.

I was inspired by his story and began to learn more about investing. I discovered that I could use the same strategies he used to reach my own financial goals. I started saving money and investing little by little, learning as I went. Over time, my investments paid off.

It was then that I realized the importance of investing in long-term wealth creation. That's why I became a passionate advocate of investing, and why I'm now delighted to share my knowledge and experience with you.

Like many of us, I was faced with a dilemma when I started exploring investment opportunities. On the one hand, I wanted to maximize my gains, but on the other, I was completely unsure of myself and afraid of making mistakes.

However, there was one thing I was 100% sure of! I had to get out of my comfort zone and learn how to navigate the investment world if I really wanted to succeed and get by!

So I decided to start investing a little at a time, taking care not to put all my eggs in one basket.

I studied the financial markets and learned from my mistakes, always bearing in mind that the key to success as an investor was continuous learning. Little by little, I began to see positive results from my investments.

I also learned the importance of diversifying my investment portfolio to minimize risk and maximize returns. I started with a PEA to invest in French shares and ETFs, which enabled me to benefit from tax advantages.

Then I realized that to go further, I needed a brokerage account.

The brokerage account has enabled me to invest in international markets, in particular the US market, which is one of the most dynamic in the world. Thanks to this increased diversification, I've been able to reduce risk and maximize returns, while gaining access to a wider range of investment opportunities.

As investors, we all have the power to create our own wealth, but this requires an understanding of the risks and opportunities we face.

Investing is a wonderful opportunity, but it can also cause irreparable damage if we don't use this tool wisely.

It's crucial not to take this book as an instruction manual, but rather as a guide to help you develop your own approach to investing. The key to being a profitable investor is continuous learning!

My aim in writing this book is to provide you with a clear and concise understanding of investing in the stock market using a brokerage account. My aim is to demystify stock market investing and enable everyone to make informed financial decisions.

I've worked hard to simplify financial concepts so that anyone can understand how to invest. My hope is that this book will be an accessible guide for investment beginners.

Today, at the age of 34, I am proud to say that I have become a seasoned investor and have created passive income streams through my investments. I'm also happy to share my knowledge with you through this book and sincerely hope to help you become financially free.

It's time to take control of your financial future. Are you ready to take action?

Your opinion counts!

Once you've finished this book, share your review. Your feedback will be useful for future readers.

I look forward to seeing how this book has impacted you.

Thank you in advance for your contribution, and happy reading!

Part 1:

The secrets of the stock market

"The only free meal,

is diversification!"

Harry Markowitz

Chapter 1:

Get rich with the stock market

1. What is the stock market?

A. Definition of the stock market

The stock market is a place where investors, like you and me, buy and sell shares in companies.

By buying a share in a company on the stock market, you become a partial owner of that company and receive part of what it earns in the form of dividends.

You can also buy these shares at a good price and sell them later at a higher price, in order to make a profit.

B. An example for a better understanding

Suppose you decide to buy shares in a company called XYZ. By purchasing these shares, you become a partial owner of the company and share in its profits and losses.

If the company performs well and its shares increase in value, you can sell your shares at a higher price than you bought them, and make a profit.

It's important to note that the stock market is a volatile market, which means that share prices fluctuate over time. That's why it's crucial to be well-informed before investing!

Rest assured, in this book you'll know it all! Together, we'll discover how the stock market can help you achieve your financial goals.

So get ready!

2. How does the stock market work?

A. Stocks/ Shares

The stock market is a way of getting rich by investing in companies that create wealth. To understand how it works, we first need to talk about stocks.

Shares are pieces of ownership in a company. When you buy a share, you become the owner of a small part of the company. You therefore have the right to share in the company's profits and decisions.

How are shares bought and sold on the stock market?

It's quite simple. Companies sell shares to raise money to grow, and investors buy shares to become owners of these companies and hope to receive future profits.

The other important aspect of the exchange's operation is the evaluation of its stocks.

How do we know how much a share costs?

That's where stock market indices come in. A stock market index is a barometer that reflects the general state of the stock market. It is constructed from a set of stocks representative of a specific economic sector or country.

Like a thermometer for measuring temperature, a stock market index measures the health and performance of the stock market as a whole. Fluctuations in the index reflect the movements of the individual stocks that make it up, and give an indication of investor sentiment and the general economic outlook.

B. ETFs

ETFs are financial products that enable investors to buy a wide range of stocks in a single purchase. Unlike individual stocks, ETFs enable investors to diversify their portfolios by buying shares in several companies at once.

ETFs generally track a stock market index, such as the S&P 500 or NASDAQ.

Here are the 10 stock market indices most often used by investors around the world:

- S&P 500 (Standard & Poor's 500) - United States
- DJIA (Dow Jones Industrial Average) - United States
- NASDAQ Composite - United States

- Nikkei 225 - Japan
- FTSE 100 - United Kingdom
- DAX 30 - Germany
- CAC 40 - France
- Hang Seng - Hong Kong
- Shanghai Composite - China
- BSE Sensex - India

When the index rises, so does the value of the ETF, allowing investors to earn money. Imagine if you had to buy every one of the 500 stocks that make up the S&P 500 index! You'd need a fortune and a lot of time to manage it all...

The advantage of ETFs is that they offer a simple, affordable way of investing in the stock market without having to buy individual stocks. ETFs are often highly liquid, meaning that investors can easily buy and sell their ETFs.

3. The advantages of investing in the stock market

A. The magic of dividends

Dividends are payments that companies make to their shareholders (you, once you've bought your first share) in proportion to their stake in the company. Dividends can be seen as interest on the investment you have made by buying shares in the company.

Imagine you've invested in a company.

When the company makes money, it gives you part of it in the form of dividends. It's a kind of "gift" to thank you for investing in their business. Dividends can be seen as a reward for your patience and trust in the company!

Dividends help you build wealth in many ways.

First of all, companies that pay regular dividends are often considered stable and financially sound, which can increase the value of your shares over the long term.

What's more, dividends allow you to receive a regular income stream without having to sell your shares, helping you build wealth over the long term.

Not all companies pay dividends, and dividends can vary according to company performance.

B. Compound interest and its power

That's right, compound interest increases your wealth at an exponential rate over the years!

Compound interest is like a snowball effect for your money. Each year, the interest earned on your money is added to your capital, and you earn interest on the whole sum the next year. Over time, the accumulated interest gets bigger and bigger!

Basically, you earn money on money you've already earned. At first, this may seem a little complicated, but the important thing to remember is that it will help you get richer and richer over time.

Do you invest in dividend-paying stocks? You receive a little extra money each year on top of the increase in the value of your shares. You can reinvest this extra money, which means you earn interest on your interest.

Over the years, this leads to exponential growth in your capital. Not for nothing did Albert Einstein say that compound interest is the 8th wonder of the world! That's why people who invested just a few tens of thousands of euros 20 or 30 years ago sometimes find themselves millionaires today!

C. Diversify your assets

One day, my 10-year-old son asked me, "Dad, why are you buying shares in a company?"

Here's what I replied:

"Imagine you have a basket with all your money in it. If you put all your money into one company, it's like putting all your money into one basket. If that business doesn't do well, then your money won't be safe and you could lose it.

Instead, if you invest in several companies, it's like putting your money in several different baskets. Even if one basket doesn't do well, you still have other baskets that can compensate for that loss and protect your money!

You can invest in the stock market at any time and anywhere in the world, which means you can choose the best opportunities for you at any time. You're no longer limited by a lot of brakes!"

Investing in the stock market offers the opportunity to diversify your assets. Instead of investing everything in a single sector, or in a single country (as is often the case with real estate investment), you can invest in shares or ETFs in different sectors and countries. You reduce your overall risk, because if one of your investments runs into difficulties, your other investments can compensate for this loss!

Finally, investing in the stock market offers you great flexibility. You can invest anywhere in the world, giving you access to a wide range of investment opportunities. You are no longer limited by the physical location of companies.

4. Golden rules for getting rich

A. Educate yourself

Knowledge is the key to success in the stock market. It's important to understand market mechanisms, the different types of shares, economic and financial indicators, and so on. In addition to this book, there are many online resources to help you learn and develop your knowledge.

Here are a few reliable French-language websites to help you develop your knowledge of stock market investing. Here are some of the best:

- Investing.com

- Morningstar
- S&P Global Ratings
- Yahoo Finance
- NASDAQ
- Motley Fool
- Seeking Alpha
- Forbes Investing

B. Set your goals

If you want to succeed in the stock market, you need to have a clear vision of what you want to achieve. To do this, I advise you to set your financial goals first.

Maybe you want to save money for a comfortable retirement. Maybe you simply want to diversify your portfolio and prepare for the future. Whatever the reason, clearly determining your goals is a crucial first step to success in the stock market. Knowing what you want to achieve will enable you to make informed decisions and direct your strategy accordingly.

Here are some questions to ask yourself to find your investment objective:

- What is my investment horizon (short, medium or long term)?
- Do I want to build wealth for retirement?
- Do I want to make investing in the stock market a passive source of income?
- Do I want to diversify to minimize risk?
- What's my risk tolerance?
- How much do I want to invest?
- Do I want to invest in ethical or sustainable causes?

C. Develop your investment strategy

Will you buy individual stocks to have more direct control over your portfolio, or would you prefer to invest in ETFs for a more diversified approach?

This choice will depend on your financial objectives, your risk tolerance and your experience of investing in the stock market.

It's crucial not to spread yourself too thin, and to choose an investment strategy that's right for you.

Every investor has different objectives and a unique risk tolerance. So it's important to take the time to think about your personal strategy.

There are many ways to invest in the stock market, but it's crucial to choose a strategy that's right for you.

I say this because, when you're just starting out, you don't necessarily realize that there are dozens and dozens of different strategies! For example, you can :

- Invest in ETFs for maximum diversification
- Investing in foreign companies
- Use options to profit from market volatility
- Invest in companies that produce goods or services on a global scale
- Invest in companies specializing in real estate (listed property companies)
- Investing in promising start-ups
- Etc.

I could go on and on! Rest assured, in the following chapters we'll look together at how to build a portfolio and strategy that's right for you.

D. Monitor your investments

Monitoring your investments is crucial to achieving your financial goals. It's important to monitor your portfolio and be ready to adjust your strategy according to market conditions. Don't let your emotions get the better of you; be objective and analytical in your approach to maximize your chances of success.

Market fluctuations can be stressful, but it's important to remain "neutral" to maximize your chances of success. Avoid getting carried away by fear when your investments go down, or by excitement when they go up. Keep your investment strategy and financial goals in mind, and don't make impulsive decisions based on spur-of-the-moment emotions.

Personally, in my brokerage account, I've been known to have stocks that fluctuate wildly.

I invested in a company called SL Green Realty Corp (ticker NYSE: SLG), which lost 51% of its value!

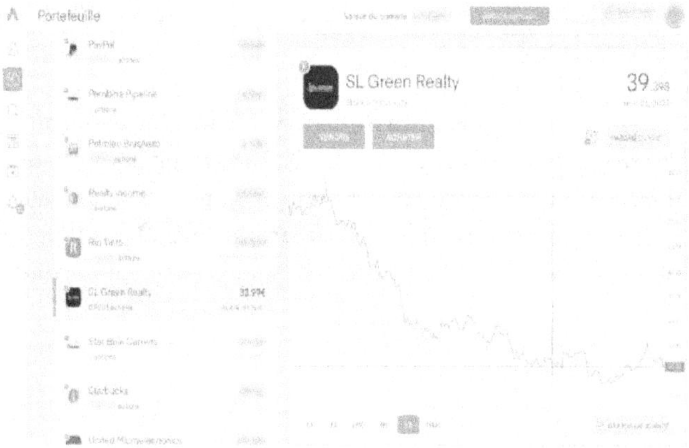

Most novice investors would have sold this position, but I kept it, because I'm convinced that over the long term, this company will continue to grow.

Indeed, this company is a major player in its sector. What's more, it's located in an area that meets a vital human need: housing. We all agree that we're not going to stop living in houses any time soon!

E. Be patient

Investing in the stock market is not a race, but a marathon!

The big winners in the stock market are those who stay in the market for many years. Patience is a virtue for success in the stock market, so stay focused on your long-term goals and don't give in to your impulses.

Warren Buffett is considered one of the greatest stock market investors of all time, and one of the richest men in the world. It goes without saying that you'll hear all about him along the way!

He is CEO of Berkshire Hathaway, a Nebraska-based multi-sector investment company. He is known for his long-term approach to investing, focused on finding undervalued companies with strong long-term growth potential. Buffett is often quoted for his sound financial and investment maxims.

Here are some of his quotes about patience in investing:

- "Investment is a long-distance race, not a sprint."
- "Patience is an essential quality for long-term investors."
- "Successful investing requires long-term patience, an absence of fear and an absence of greed."
- "The secret to success in the stock market is to set clear goals and not let emotions influence your decisions."

Investing in the stock market can take time to generate significant returns, so be patient and stay focused on your long-term goals!

5. What influences the stock market?

A. The policy

Government decisions

The impact of government policies on the stock market should not be ignored. Decisions taken by governments sometimes have a direct impact on companies. For example, a reduction in public spending can lead to a drop in demand for certain products and services, which in turn can have an impact on corporate profits.

Similarly, new regulations can increase costs for some companies.

Example

A government announces a reduction in public spending, particularly in the transport sector.

This announcement will have an impact on companies supplying public transport equipment. With the reduction in public spending in this area, these companies will suffer a drop in orders and therefore see their profits fall...

B. The Fed

A definition is in order

The Fed, or Federal Reserve, is the central bank of the United States. It is responsible for monetary policy, which means that it manages the amount of money in circulation in the US economy. The Fed is also responsible for regulating the financial system. In short, it is a very important institution for the American economy and for financial markets worldwide!

The Fed...

This American central bank has a huge impact on the world's stock markets. You can't imagine how investors around the world are watching their every move.

Indeed, when the Fed takes measures such as raising interest rates, it triggers chain reactions on the world's stock markets. Investors can become nervous and quickly sell their shares, which can lead to a fall in prices.

On the other hand, if the Fed takes measures that support the economy, such as injecting liquidity or lowering interest rates, this can stimulate economic growth and support stock markets.

In short, the Fed is a key player in the world of finance, and its decisions have a major impact on global stock markets. Investors therefore need to pay close attention to their movements to make informed investment decisions.

C. Economic conditions

Recession, when you hold us...

If a country's economy is in recession, companies see their sales and profits fall, which often leads to a drop in their stock market value...

Take, for example, the current economic situation in France. With COVID-19, the French economy went into recession, resulting in a drop in demand for many products and services. Companies that depend on household consumption, such as retail stores, were particularly hard hit. Shares in these companies fell accordingly.

Is there any way to avoid this problem?

Yes, there is a way!

By investing in companies that can withstand difficult economic conditions, you can minimize the risks to your portfolio.

You'll understand why I invite you to ask yourself the following questions in Chapter 4:

- Is the company in a position to cope with an economic downturn (health crisis, international crisis, etc.)?

- Is the company diversified and does it sell worldwide?

By asking yourself these questions and choosing your stock market assets accordingly, you can minimize the impact of economic conditions!

Chapter 2:

Everything you need to know about brokerage account

1. Definitions

The brokerage account allows you to buy and sell stocks, bonds, and other financial products. It is generally used by investors who frequently trade U.S. or international securities.

2. Advantages and disadvantages

A. Advantages

- Flexibility: this account allows you to invest in a wide variety of international shares, offering greater diversification and the chance to take advantage of investment opportunities around the world. There are many countries offering very attractive returns and opportunities not found in Europe...

- No investment ceiling: the brokerage account has no investment ceiling, so you can invest as much as you like!

- Free management: unlike well-known life insurance contracts, the brokerage account offers greater management freedom, allowing you to customize your portfolio according to your investment objectives and risk profile.

B. Disadvantages

- Withholding tax on capital gains.
- No tax reduction for this investment.
- Less protection in the event of bankruptcy. This disadvantage needs to be qualified, as it depends on the jurisdiction of the broker who holds your brokerage account. If you use American or British brokers, there is less "chance" of finding yourself in a bankruptcy situation. Moreover, there's nothing 100% certain in life!

4. Who can open a brokerage account?

A. Eligibility criteria by country

In the US

In general, eligibility criteria include :

- Be of legal age in the state of residence
- Valid proof of identity
- Have a mailing address in the US
- Have a valid social insurance number

- Meet credit history check requirements

In Canada

In Canada, the criteria may vary by province or territory. In general, eligibility criteria include :

- Be of legal age in the province or territory of residence
- Valid proof of identity
- Have a mailing address in Canada
- Have a valid social insurance number
- Meet credit history check requirements

In Australia

In Australia, the criteria may vary by territory. In general, eligibility criteria include :

- Must be of legal age in the state of residence.
- Valid proof of identity
- Have a mailing address in Australia

- Provide an Australian Tax File Number (TFN) – while not mandatory, it can ensure you are not overtaxed.

- Meet credit history check requirements

In the U.K

The criteria may vary by territory. In general, eligibility criteria include :

- Must be at least 18 years old.

- Valid proof of identity

- Have a U.K. mailing address.

- Provide a National Insurance Number

- Meet credit history check requirements

B. Please note that conditions may vary!

Eligibility criteria for opening a brokerage account vary according to the country in which you live.

Changing conditions may be related to :

- minimum age requirement,

- nationality,
- the residence,
- minimum deposit requirements,
- etc.

Take the time to check these details with your financial institution. And don't forget that laws change!

What's more, although I've done extensive research, I'm not a tax lawyer or legal expert! It's up to you to do your own research, or to enlist the help of a professional if necessary.

C. Deposit guarantee fund

The deposit guarantee fund is an institution that protects investors in the event of the bankruptcy of their broker or bank. The deposit guarantee fund varies according to the broker and/or the laws in force in the country.

In the United States, depositors in US banks are protected by the Federal Deposit Insurance Corporation (FDIC). The FDIC guarantees up to $250 000 USD per depositor, per insured bank, for each account ownership category.

In Canada, each province has its own deposit guarantee fund. For example, « Quebec's Autorité des marchés financiers » manages the Federal Deposit, which guarantees up to $100 000 CAD per person and per financial institution.

In Australia, the Financial Claims Scheme (FCS) acts as a safety net for depositors in Australian incorporated banks, building societies, and credit unions. Managed by the Australian Prudential Regulation Authority (APRA), it guarantees up to $250 000 AUD per account holder, per financial institution.

In the United Kingdom, the Financial Services Compensation Scheme (FSCS) ensures that depositors are protected if a bank or building society goes out of business. Depositors can rest assured that their deposits are covered up to £85 000 GBP per person, per financial institution. For joint accounts, this coverage extends up to £170 000 GBP.

Chapter 3:

Understanding stocks and ETFs made easy

---

1. The shares

A. How do stocks generate wealth?

To understand how stocks generate wealth, it's important to understand how companies create wealth.

A company creates wealth by producing and/or selling products or services that are demanded by consumers.

If a company makes a profit, it will tend to attract more investors, which can increase the value of its shares.

For example, if a company has high earnings and is growing fast, investors will be willing to pay a higher price for its shares.

However, this isn't always the case, and as with everything in life, it's important to keep things in perspective!

Take Spotify, for example. Although it's very popular with users, its business model doesn't yet allow it to turn a profit.

And yet, the price of its shares has risen and fallen with the market's enthusiasm for the company. Bear in mind that share price trends do not always reflect the company's financial health. It's best to avoid blindly following trends and do your own research before investing in a company.

As you can see, the bottom line (the company's net profit) is catastrophic (red box).

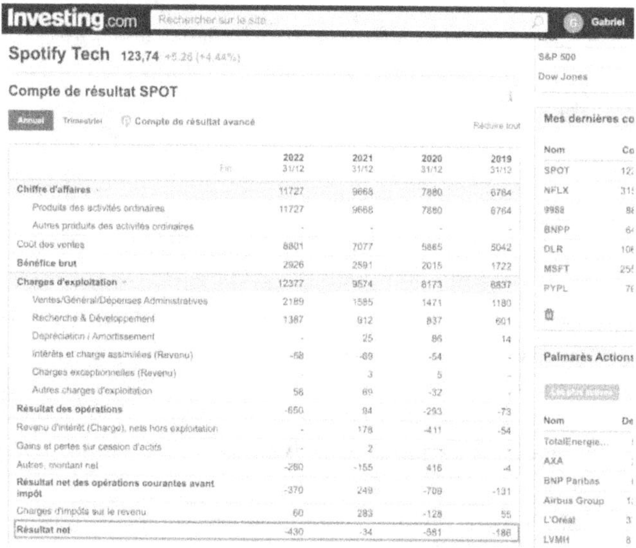

Spotify Tech 123,74 +5.26 (+4.44%)

Compte de résultat SPOT

Annuel Trimestriel Compte de résultat avancé Réduire tout

Fin	2022 31/12	2021 31/12	2020 31/12	2019 31/12
Chiffre d'affaires	11727	9668	7880	6764
Produits des activités ordinaires	11727	9668	7880	6764
Autres produits des activités ordinaires	-	-	-	-
Coût des ventes	8801	7077	5865	5042
Bénéfice brut	2926	2591	2015	1722
Charges d'exploitation	12377	9574	8173	6837
Ventes/Général/Dépenses Administratives	2189	1585	1471	1180
Recherche & Développement	1387	912	837	601
Dépréciation / Amortissement	-	25	86	14
Intérêts et charge assimilées (Revenu)	-68	-69	-54	-
Charges exceptionnelles (Revenu)	-	3	5	-
Autres charges d'exploitation	56	69	-32	-
Résultat des opérations	-650	94	-293	-73
Revenu d'intérêt (Charge), nets hors exploitation	-	178	-411	-54
Gains et pertes sur cession d'actifs	-	2	-	-
Autres, montant net	-280	-155	416	-4
Résultat net des opérations courantes avant impôt	-370	249	-709	-131
Charges d'impôts sur le revenu	60	283	-128	55
Résultat net	-430	-34	-581	-186

B. The advantages and disadvantages of shares

The benefits of shares

- Growth: shares enable investors to invest in companies that are growing, leading to an increase in share value over time, and therefore in their capital!

- Dividends: Dividends are a source of income for investors. They are also an effective means of significantly increasing investors' long-term capital, thanks to the effect of compound interest.

- Diversification: shares enable investors to diversify their portfolios and reduce their overall risk. In fact, you can buy shares from any country in the world!

- Liquidity: shares are considered liquid assets, which means they are easy to buy and sell on the financial markets. This is not the case with some other investments, such as real estate, where you have to wait months before you can sell your property!

- Long-term wealth creation: shares are often seen as a long-term purchase and are a good way to build wealth over the long term!

The disadvantages of shares

- Financial risks: investing in shares entails financial risks, as companies may suffer losses or decline in business.

- Volatility: some stocks are volatile, meaning that their values vary considerably over the course of a single day or even a few hours. But don't worry, we'll look at how to minimize your risk in the next chapter, so that your investments are as profitable as possible.

- Liquidity: some stocks (those of small companies) can be difficult to sell quickly. Don't worry, if you follow the criteria I'll give you next, you won't be bothered by liquidity problems.

- Complexity: it's sometimes difficult for beginners to understand corporate financial information. But I'm here to make it easier for you.

C. Differences between large and small company shares

Shares in major companies

Large-cap stocks are generally considered more stable for the following reasons:

- They belong to established companies with a track record of successful financial performance.

- They often have customers in several countries around the world, as they are truly multinationals.

- They have considerable cash flow, substantial assets and products/services that are widely known in the marketplace.

However, the growth potential of large company shares is often more limited than that of small companies for the following reasons:

- They have often already reached a certain maturity in the market, which can make expansion more difficult.
- Decisions take longer to be taken in these companies due to their complex hierarchical structure.

Small company shares

Small-cap stocks are often considered to have higher growth potential than large-cap stocks. This is largely due to their room for growth.

However, this growth potential is often accompanied by higher risk, as these companies do not yet have a "good financial track record". As their financial future is still uncertain, investing in these stocks is riskier.

D. Growth vs. dividend!

What's the difference?

Broadly speaking, there are 2 types of shares you can buy on the stock market:

1. growth stocks

2. dividend stocks

The differences between the 2 may seem subtle, but they are very important in understanding their performance potential.

Growth stocks are shares in companies that are still investing heavily in their development to grow and expand their business. In general, they have not yet begun to distribute dividends to shareholders, but this is not true in all cases. They may have greater potential to increase in value.

Here are a few examples you're probably familiar with:

- Apple
- Amazon
- Facebook
- Tesla
- Netflix
- Uber
- Airbnb
- Zoom

In this list, only Apple pays dividends to its shareholders!

Dividend stocks, on the other hand, are shares in more established companies that regularly distribute a portion of their profits to shareholders in the form of dividends. This type of stock offers a regular source of income, but its value generally doesn't grow as much as growth stocks.

Here are a few examples you're probably familiar with:

- The Coca-Cola Company
- Chevron
- Procter & Gamble
- Mc Donald's Corporation
- Home Depot
- Johnson & Johnson

Looking for a regular source of income?
→ Dividend stocks are a smart choice!

Want to bet on a stock's rise in value?
→ Growth stocks are better for you!

My advice

In the beginning, I recommend that you concentrate on dividend stocks. These companies are much more established, and you're less likely to lose your capital.

When you're more confident, you can buy growth stocks.

No action is better than another. It just depends on your strategy. Personally, I own more dividend stocks than growth stocks, but I invest in both!

E. Obligations

I'm not going to say too much about them, as they're not financial assets that I use. But I will give you a quick introduction to this type of investment.

Bonds are financial securities issued by governments or companies.

How do they work?

You lend money to the bond issuer for a specified period. At the end of this period, the issuer repays your capital with interest. Bonds are considered safer than stocks, because they offer a fixed, guaranteed rate of interest.

However, bonds also present risks. If the bond issuer can't repay the loan, you lose your principal. What's more, if interest rates rise, bonds lose value. So it's important to pay attention to the quality of the bond issuer before making an investment.

As I mentioned earlier, I'm not a big fan of bonds and rarely use them in my investment portfolio.

2. ETFs

A. What are ETFs and how do they work?

What is an ETF?

An ETF (Exchange-Traded Fund) is an exchange-traded fund that allows investors to acquire a basket of assets, such as stocks, bonds or commodities, without having to buy them individually.

ETFs are often used to diversify a portfolio, and their structure makes them easy to buy and sell on the stock market.

How do they work?

They are attractive to those looking to diversify their investment portfolio without the headache.

ETFs are managed by a fund management company. ETF shares are then sold to investors on the various stock exchanges.

ETFs are traded like ordinary shares, which means that investors can buy and sell them at any time during trading hours.

What's more, ETFs are often less expensive than traditional mutual funds, as they don't require high management fees, making them an advantageous option for all investors.

B. The advantages and disadvantages of ETFs

The advantages of ETFs

- Low cost: because of their simple structure, they are generally less expensive than mutual funds.

- Flexibility: ETFs can be bought or sold at any time during stock market trading hours, making them a flexible option for investors.

- Diversification: they enable investors to diversify their portfolios by investing in a wide range of assets, thereby reducing risk.

- Transparency: ETF managers are required by law to publish regular information about their ETFs, so investors know exactly where their money is.

- Ease of use: they are accessible to investment beginners.

The disadvantages of ETFs

- Additional charges: some ETFs may have additional charges such as management fees, transaction fees and tracking fees, which reduce the total investment return.

- Limited liquidity: some ETFs have limited liquidity, making it difficult to sell quickly when needed.

- Misalignments: they may be subject to misalignments if the assets have not been correctly tracked by the managers, which may result in a loss of value for the investor.

C. How to invest in ETFs

1. Evaluate your investor profile: determine your investment objectives, risk tolerance and time horizon.

2. Look for ETFs that match your investment objectives.

3. Buy ETFs: once you've opened your CTO, you can buy ETFs directly.

4. Once you've bought ETFs, monitor your portfolio regularly and adapt your strategy to suit your objectives.

Note that ETF investments are subject to brokerage fees and other costs, so it's important to consider these before making an investment decision.

Chapter 4:

Finding the best stocks

---

1. Fundamental company analysis

A. What are the key indicators to monitor?

In my opinion, the study of financial performance is the basis of the stock selection process.

Take the time to "do your homework", examine the company and make sure you understand it before making a decision. This is key to finding the best stocks for your portfolio, and will help you avoid taking unnecessary risks.

Often, when we talk about the key indicators to watch when assessing a company's financial performance, we hear about sales, net income, profit margins, sales growth, financial situation (liquidity, debt), return on assets and shares. In my opinion, however, there are far more relevant indicators for determining whether or not I'm interested in a stock.

B. The key indicators I use to invest

An indicator (also known as a ratio) represents a financial characteristic of a company.

Investors use them to make informed decisions before investing.

Here are some questions to ask yourself before focusing on financial ratios:

- Do I understand the products and services the company offers?
- Am I confident that the company will remain operational in 20 years?
- Does the company possess a lasting competitive edge?
- Is the company equipped to withstand economic challenges such as wars, health crises, international disputes, and the like?
- Is the company's business diversified, with global sales reach?

Once you've asked yourself these questions, you can move on to the study of ratios.

I'd like to make it clear that there is no "right or wrong" answer. Some investors can easily understand the services offered by a company, while others cannot. Some investors are convinced that a stock will still be around in 20 years' time, while others are not.

Let's move on to the study of ratios. To help you, here's the list I use to determine whether or not to invest in a stock!

Capitalization in excess of $500 million

Market capitalization is a key indicator of a company's market value. For example, if a company has 1 million shares outstanding and the share price is $50, its market capitalization would be $50 million (1 million shares x $50 per share).

A company with a market capitalization of over $500 million is considered more solid because it has a greater number of shares outstanding, which means greater financial stability and a better ability to generate income.

Companies with a high market capitalization generally have a strong financial track record. This indicator is only one element to consider, and it is important to consult other financial data to make an informed investment decision.

That's just what we're going to see next!

More than 5% dividends paid each year

Investing in stocks that pay regular dividends is a way of generating passive income over the long term.

In fact, if you receive dividends every year and reinvest them in the share, you benefit from the compounding effect, which considerably increases your capital over the long term.

That's why I consider stocks paying dividends of over 5% a year to be more attractive for my portfolio!

No dividend cuts or reductions for at least 5 years

Regular dividend payments are a key indicator of a company's financial performance.

Companies that have been paying dividends for at least 5 years without interruption or reduction are more reliable. The company has enough profits to continue growing, while continuing to distribute a portion of its profits to investors!

The longer a company has been paying dividends, the more reliable and high quality it is regarded as by investors.

Dividends king

Dividends king are companies that have increased their dividends every year for at least 50 years!

Dividend king companies are solid, established and recognized businesses. They are attractive to investors looking to generate regular income.

Here is a non-exhaustive list of dividend king companies:

- Johnson & Johnson (JNJ)
- Procter & Gamble Co (PG)
- Coca-Cola Co. (KO)

- PepsiCo Inc (PEP)
- Walmart Inc (WMT)
- Colgate-Palmolive Co (CL)
- ExxonMobil Corp (XOM)
- Chevron Corp (CVX)
- AT&T Inc (T)

At the time of writing, some companies may have dropped out of the rankings, while others may have moved up. It's up to you to check!

Even "dividend king" companies may one day run into financial difficulties, or cut their dividends due to economic downturns. When this happens, the company is no longer classified as a "dividend king".

So it's up to you to keep an eye on these companies!

Constant dividend growth of at least +4%/year

A constant dividend growth rate of at least +4% per year is an important indicator of a company's ability to maintain a high level of dividend payments over time.

This rate testifies to the company's ability to maintain a solid financial performance, demonstrating its capacity to continue paying dividends to its shareholders at a rate that has steadily increased over the years.

Investing in a company that cannot maintain constant dividend growth is risky in the long term.

A payout ratio of less than 60%.

The payout ratio is calculated by dividing the dividends paid by the company by its net income.

Example

A company makes a net profit of $500 000 and decides to adopt a payout ratio of 50%. Total dividends paid will be $250 000.

→ $500 000 x 50 % = $250 000

The payout ratio is 50%, which means that the company pays out 50% of its net income in the form of dividends.

A ratio of less than 60% indicates that the company is not paying out too much of its profits in the form of dividends, allowing it to retain enough cash to grow.

However, there is one exception! This exception applies to listed property companies, which need to retain a higher proportion of their profits to buy real estate, as this type of company requires more equity to carry out its activities.

Note that this can also be the case for companies in the healthcare sector with large equity capital requirements, linked to medical research.

Precision

Listed property companies are companies that invest in real estate and are listed on the stock exchange. They buy and manage real estate, such as buildings, houses, offices, shopping centers or apartments, to generate rental income. Shares in these companies are attractive for investors who want to "buy real estate" without the drawbacks!

A PER of between 3 and 25

The Price Earning Ratio (PER) is an indicator that measures the relationship between a company's share price and earnings per share (EPS).

Example

A company's share price is $100 and its earnings per share (EPS) is $5. In this case, the company's P/E would be 20 ($100 / $5 = 20). This means that the market is willing to pay 20 times the company's earnings per share.

Comparing this with another company with a share price of $50 and EPS of $5, the P/E would be 10 ($50 / $5 = 10). In this case, the company with a lower PER may appear more attractive to investors, as the market is willing to pay less for each unit of profit generated by the company.

I recommend that you take other factors into account and don't make an investment decision based on PER alone!

I'm looking to invest in shares with a P/E of between 3 and 25.

A P/E below 3 may mean that the company is in difficulty or may not be profitable, while a P/E above 25 may mean that the company is "overvalued".

A PER of between 3 and 25 is a good compromise. It allows you to find stocks with good value for money, while avoiding those considered too expensive or risky.

A margin greater than 13% before tax

A company has sales of $500 000 and pre-tax profits of $75 000.

Rest assured, you won't have to do all the calculations, because a site like Investing.com already does them for you!

Here is the formula for calculating the pre-tax margin rate:

(Profit before tax / Sales) x 100

In our example, the pre-tax margin is :

($75 000 / $500 000) x 100 = 15 %

For each euro of sales, the company makes a gross profit of 15 centimes.

If a company doesn't have enough margin to cover its costs, chances are it won't be able to make a profit. As a result, it is likely to stop paying dividends...

Why 13% and no other figure?

When researching and listening to some of the world's leading investors, this is a figure that often comes up.

Less than 70% debt-to-equity ratio

A company's debt-to-equity ratio measures the proportion of debt to equity.

A debt-to-equity ratio of over 70% is an indicator of a risky business. In fact, it means that the company has too much debt. Unfortunately, the company may have difficulty repaying its debts or generating profits, which means there's a greater risk of not receiving dividends, or even worse, of losing your initial investment, if the company goes bankrupt!

The exception is listed property companies, which are often more indebted due to the purchase of real estate. Thus, for listed property companies, a higher debt ratio is acceptable, as they have tangible assets of great value to compensate.

That's why it's important to consider the debt ratio in the context of each individual company.

Net income up for 3 consecutive years

This is an important indicator of a company's financial health. It shows that the company is growing and profitable.

This indicator is a positive sign that the company will be able to continue generating profits in the future. Many investors tend to overlook this ratio. Yet it is crucial, as it shows that the company has the capacity to maintain or increase dividend payments!

Beta between 0 and 0.5 over 10 years (optional)

Beta measures a stock's volatility relative to the market as a whole. A beta value between 0 and 0.5 means that the stock is less sensitive to market fluctuations than the market as a whole.

This can be seen as relevant for investors seeking to minimize their risk over the long term by choosing stocks less exposed to economic cycles.

A company makes the borrowed money grow at 5% min (optional)

If a company borrows money at an interest rate of 2% and is able to make that borrowed money grow at a rate of at least 5%, that means it makes a gain of 3% on every euro borrowed!

For example, if she borrows $100 000 at an interest rate of 2%, she will pay $2 000 in interest per year.

If she invests the borrowed money in a project with a 5% return, she earns $5 000 a year. The net gain on this loan will therefore be $3 000 per year ($5 000 - $2 000).

C. Caution!

I don't want my readers to find themselves in a bad financial situation.

This list is not a miracle checklist! It should not be taken as a magic wand that will automatically find you companies to invest in!

Always bear in mind that there are other factors you can take into account. Sometimes, I leave a tiny bit of room (and I do mean a tiny bit) for my instincts.

It may sound strange, but common sense can be a good ally. When it comes to money and investing, I recommend that you always stand back and take a nuanced view of what you read. For example, just because a stock has performed well doesn't necessarily mean it will continue to do so in the future!

Nobody reads crystal balls! So I recommend that you shun advice from people who tell you that investing in stocks, ETFs or any other asset is 100% safe.

Generally speaking, when it's too good to be true, it's too good to be true!

2. Technical analysis

A. Graphs and market trends

Technical analysis is an approach that uses historical stock price and volume data to anticipate future price movements. For investors using this method, stock charts are key tools for understanding market trends.

Imagine you're in a soccer stadium and you're watching the ball go from player to player. You can see the movements and tendencies of each player.

Similarly, by analyzing stock charts, you can see movements and trends in the price and volume of these stocks.

Investors using technical analysis look for recurring patterns and trends in charts to determine the best investment opportunities. They can use indicators such as moving averages, Bollinger bands and momentum indicators to make more informed decisions.

B. Technical indicators

Technical indicators are mathematical tools that use historical data on stock price and volume to help predict future trends.

Using these technical indicators, we can assess the market trend, identify support and resistance levels and detect buy and sell signals. It's like having a radar that lets you know where stock prices are heading.

Technical analysis is not an exact science, and there is no guarantee of the accuracy of its forecasts.

By combining technical analysis with sound fundamental analysis, and by being patient and disciplined in our investment decisions, we can improve our results.

If you want to be a smart investor, it's important to be able to read charts and use technical indicators to evaluate stocks. This is a key element in increasing your chances of success on the stock market.

C. My point of view on technical analysis

I think technical analysis is too complicated for investment beginners. In my opinion, fundamental analysis is more relevant for finding good stocks.

Personally, I've never felt the need to use technical analysis to make sound investment decisions in my brokerage account.

Looking back, the performance of my brokerage account proved me right!

I prefer to rely on fundamental analysis to find solid long-term stocks, rather than complicated charts and indicators. To each his own, but for me, technical analysis is simply not necessary.

Technical analysis is best suited to short-term traders. It doesn't concern us in this book, as we're concentrating on medium- and long-term investments. That's why I don't go into more detail on this type of analysis.

Chapter 5:

Find the best ETFs

---

1. Why ETFs are attractive to investors

A. Who created ETFs and why?

ETFs (Exchange Traded Funds) were first created in the USA in the 1970s by the investment firms State Street Global Advisors and American Stock Exchange.

ETFs were created to provide investors with an easily accessible, low-cost investment option for diversifying their portfolios.

ETFs allow investors to benefit from exposure to a basket of stocks, bonds, gold or other assets, without having to buy each one individually. ETFs have become very popular for their convenience, transparency and accessibility for both novice and experienced investors.

B. Why are ETFs attractive to novice investors?

ETFs are particularly attractive for novice investors, as they offer a simple and affordable way to diversify without having to select each stock individually.

Imagine if you had to buy all 500 stocks in the S&P 500. It would require a colossal budget and extremely time-consuming management...

What's more, ETFs are quoted in real time and are subject to relatively low management fees, making them attractive to investors looking to maximize their returns.

2. Criteria for choosing the best ETFs

A. Historical performance

Relying on what really happened

In the world of finance, it's important not just to rely on what's been said, but on what's actually happened. That's where historical performance comes in.

In other words, how have the stocks included in the ETF performed over the years?

Example

Take, for example, the most popular S&P 500 ETF, the SPDR S&P 500 ETF Trust (ticker SPY).

If we look at its performance over the past 30 years, we can see that it has enjoyed stable, steady growth, despite occasional declines.

I'm now going to show you how ETFs can literally explode your wealth when they're well selected.

→ As you can see, the return is 819% over 30 years, which is still an average annual return of 27.3%!

If you too would like to easily see ETF and stock trends, I recommend Google Finance (this image comes from Google Finance).

<u>Precision</u>

When choosing an ETF, it's important to analyze its historical performance to determine whether it's on an upward or downward trend. If you find that the fund has experienced consistent growth over a long period, this may be a sign that this ETF could be a good option for your investment portfolio.

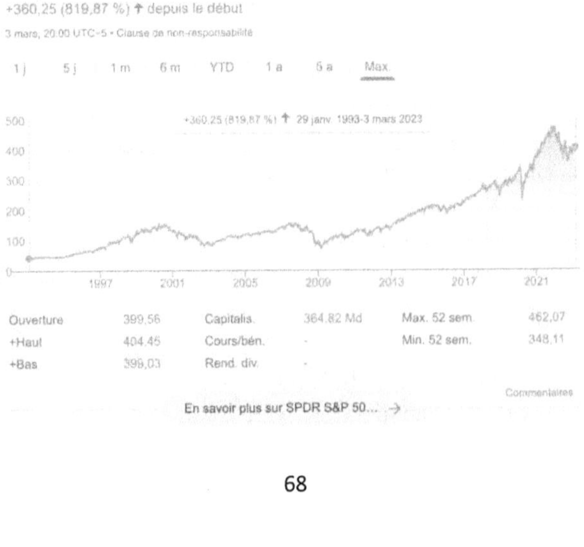

B. Distributing ETF or accumulating ETF?

You can choose between 2 main types of ETF:

- distributing ETFs
- accumulating ETFs

Distributing ETFs pay a dividend on a regular basis, usually quarterly. You receive regular income, similar to what you might receive by investing in shares.

Accumulating ETFs, on the other hand, do not pay dividends.

Instead, the gains are reinvested in the fund, leading to ETF growth through compound interest!

The choice between a distributing ETF and a accumulating ETF will depend on your personal and financial situation, as well as your investment objectives.

Looking to generate regular income?

→ Distributing ETFs are for you.

Want to maximize your portfolio's growth?

→ Accumulating ETFs are your best option.

C. Fees and commissions

An impact on your profitability

As with any investment, fees and commissions have a considerable impact on your long-term profitability. When choosing an ETF, I recommend that you pay close attention to fees.

ETFs are often sold with annual management fees ranging from 0.1% to 0.5% or more. That may not sound like much, but these fees quickly eat into your long-term performance.

How to earn $300 in just 1 minute?

Let's say you've invested $10,000 in an ETF with an annual fee of 0.5%.

After 10 years, you'll have paid $500 in fees!

Take another ETF with an annual fee of 0.2%.

If you had invested the same $10 000, you would have paid only $200 in fees over 10 years. That's a saving of $300 compared to the ETF with annual fees of 0.5%...

How do you earn $3 000 in just 1 minute?

Now, let's imagine you've invested not $10 000, but $100 000 in this ETF with an annual fee of 0.5%.

You would have paid $5 000 in costs over 10 years...

If you had chosen the ETF with an annual fee of 0.2%, you would have paid $2 000 in fees and will save $3 000 in fees over 10 years compared with the first ETF.

This demonstration perfectly illustrates the importance of paying attention to annual fee percentages!

→ My advice is to give maximum preference to ETFs with fees of the order of 0.3% or less.

Comparison with traditional funds

ETF fees are very often lower than those of traditional manager-managed funds. The fees of these funds often exceed 1% or more, while the fees of most ETFs are often less than 0.5%!

D. Diversification

Most novice investors are looking to minimize their risk and spread their investment over several business sectors, geographical regions and asset classes.

This is where ETFs come in. They enable investors to easily diversify their portfolios by purchasing a financial product that includes dozens, or even hundreds, of different stocks.

To be sure you're making the right choice, you need to be vigilant about ETF quality.

Look at the different business sectors, geographic regions and asset classes represented in the ETF. You want to be sure that the ETF is not overly focused on a single sector, region or asset class.

In short, diversification is a crucial element in choosing the best ETFs. Make sure you understand the ETF's composition before you buy!

E. Market capitalization in excess of $100 million

The amount of assets under management is an important consideration when investing in an ETF. An ETF with more than $100 million under management is considered more stable, as it has a larger investor base, which means greater liquidity and a better ability to track the index!

ETFs with large assets under management are generally more solid!

F. ETF issuers

BlackRock and Vanguard are 2 of the best-known ETF issuers on the market. They offer a variety of investment options, from exchange-traded ETFs to thematic ETFs.

BlackRock

In 2022, BlackRock became the world's largest asset manager, **with $8 487 billion in assets under management**!

BlackRock offers a wide range of products, from ETFs linked to various sectors and markets, to shares, bonds and commodities.

BlackRock is a company that does not depend on any other financial institution for its management.

BlackRock is headquartered in New York.

Vanguard

Vanguard is a well-established asset management company, offering a wide range of investment products, including ETFs, stocks, bonds, derivatives and more.

Vanguard has a well-established reputation in asset management. Founded in 1975, it is one of the world's largest asset managers, with over $7 000 billion in assets under management!

They have an investment philosophy focused on diversification, and are known for offering low-cost investment products.

3. How to assess the quality of an ETF

A. The fundamentals

To find the best ETFs, you need to know what's behind the ETF!

Here are a few questions I like to ask myself, to assess the quality of an ETF before including it in my brokerage account:

- Which sectors are represented in the ETF portfolio?
- Is there excessive concentration in a single sector or company?
- How are the companies included in the ETF chosen?
- What is the ETF's historical performance?
- How does it compare with other similar ETFs?
- What is the risk associated with ETFs?
- What are the fees associated with ETFs?

B. Assessing the quality of companies included in the ETF

To assess the quality of an ETF, it's important to consider the quality of the companies included in it. You want to be sure that you're investing in sound, financially healthy companies.

However, don't forget that the purpose of an ETF is to simplify investment. So, while the profitability of the underlying companies is important, it's not necessary to spend too much time analyzing each company individually!

Here are a few criteria to consider:

- Profitability: take a quick look at companies' net profits, their growth rates and their ability to generate profits on a regular basis.
- Debt: briefly assess the company's level of debt.
- Product or service quality: make sure that companies offer quality products or services that are in demand in the marketplace.
- Growth prospects: take a look at companies' growth opportunities, particularly in their sector and on international markets.

As our friend Warren Buffett once said, "Never invest in a company you can't understand!".

4. The best ETFs

A. Market ETFs

Market ETFs are designed to reflect the performance of the overall market or of a specific sector. They offer investment diversification and access to a large number of stocks at relatively low cost.

They are often used to invest in popular indices.

The most widely used stock market indices in the world are American...

1. The S&P 500, which tracks the 500 largest companies listed on U.S. stock exchanges.

2. The NASDAQ 100, which tracks U.S.-listed technology and growth companies.

3. The Dow Jones Industrial Average, which reflects the 30 largest industrial companies listed on the US stock exchange.

Other stock market indices

The MSCI World Index tracks the shares of large and medium-sized companies in 23 developed countries:

- Germany
- Australia
- Austria
- Belgium

- Canada
- Denmark
- Spain
- United States
- Finland
- France
- Hong Kong
- Ireland
- Israel
- Italy
- Japan
- New Zealand
- Norway
- Netherlands
- Portugal
- United Kingdom
- Singapore
- Sweden

- Switzerland

The FTSE All-World Index, which reflects the shares of large and medium-sized companies in 46 developed and emerging countries.

The Nikkei 225 tracks Japan's 225 largest listed companies.

B. Sector ETFs

Sector ETFs, also known as thematic ETFs, enable investors to focus on a particular sector of the economy.

Here is a list of economic sectors that can be found in sector ETFs:

- Technology: companies specializing in the design, manufacture and distribution of technological and electronic products.

- Healthcare: companies involved in the research and development of pharmaceutical products, healthcare services, medical equipment and medical information technologies.

- Consumer services: non-cyclical consumer goods businesses, such as food, beverages, household products, personal care and leisure.

- Financial services: banking, insurance, brokerage, asset management and other financial services companies.

- Energy: companies involved in the production, refining, storage and distribution of oil and gas, as well as other renewable energy sources.

- Materials: companies involved in the production and supply of commodities such as metals, chemicals and building materials.

- Industry: companies involved in the manufacture of durable and non-durable goods, such as machinery, aerospace, vehicles and consumer durables.

- Ect.

This approach is advantageous for investors seeking to maximize growth opportunities in a particular sector.

If you want to focus on a particular sector, I recommend choosing a sector ETF that features a wide range of companies in the sector.

Your opinion really counts!

I would be honored to see your honest review.

You help make this book better for future readers.

Tell us what you liked and what could be improved.

Thank you in advance for your contribution!

Part 2:

Fully mastering your brokerage account

"Never depend on one income. Make an investment to create a second source."

Warren Buffett

Chapter 6:

Create your own profitable portfolio

---

1. Your investment strategy

A. Determine your financial goals

Like any good investor, you must first determine your financial objectives.

- Do you want to build comfortable savings for your retirement?
- Do you want to accumulate wealth so that you can live off your investments in the future?
- Do you want to generate regular income to live on?
- Would you rather take risks to maximize potential gains?

These objectives will determine how you build your portfolio.

When you're young and don't have family responsibilities, it can make sense to focus on riskier investments with greater earning potential, in order to accumulate more wealth. This is known as the accumulation phase.

Conversely, if you're approaching retirement, it's wiser to focus on security and stability by investing in less risky and volatile assets.

Determining your financial goals is a crucial step in building a successful portfolio, so take the time to think about what you want to achieve over the long term and make sure your investments reflect those goals!

B. Assess your level of risk

There is one immutable law in investing:

→ The higher the level of risk, the greater the potential gains!

I recommend that you get to know your level of risk before building your investment portfolio.

To assess your level of risk, ask yourself the following questions:

- Am I prepared to take risks to earn more money?
- Would I prefer a more cautious approach?
- How often am I prepared to make adjustments to my portfolio?

Be careful not to underestimate the risk, as this could result in considerable losses.

Risk tolerance is a personal thing, so it's up to you to decide what you're prepared to accept!

2. Asset allocation

A. Balancing shares, ETFs and cash

Asset allocation is a key step in developing a sound investment strategy. It involves determining the proportion of your portfolio to be allocated to different asset classes, such as shares, ETFs and cash.

The aim is to find a balance that suits your tolerable level of risk and your financial objectives.

To put it more bluntly, here's what we have in mind:

- Shares offer high returns, but they are also more volatile and higher-risk.

- ETFs, on the other hand, are generally more stable and less risky, but their returns are lower.

- Liquid assets, such as savings accounts, pay little or no interest.

Asset allocation should not be static. I recommend that you review it once a year and adjust it according to your situation. Unless you already have substantial assets (over $250 000), you don't need to review your asset allocation more often.

B. Diversification

Sector diversification

Sector diversification means spreading your investments across different sectors, such as technology, healthcare, real estate, defense, energy and so on.

So if a sector doesn't perform well, you don't lose out!

Take the healthcare and IT sectors, for example.

The healthcare sector is generally less volatile, because healthcare is essential. It is always in demand, regardless of the state of the economy!

On the other hand, the IT sector is more volatile due to its dependence on economic growth and technological innovation.

By diversifying into these 2 sectors, you reduce your exposure to risk and maximize your chances of success!

Geographic diversification

Geographic diversification means spreading your investments across different countries.

So if a country's economy is in trouble, it won't affect your entire portfolio!

Imagine:

You have invested in an Australian company that is experiencing an economic slowdown...

You've also invested in a Brazilian company whose shares are booming.

Thanks to the Brazilian company's shares, your portfolio stays in the green. Geographic diversification allows you to better manage investment risk!

Currency diversification

Currency diversification involves investing in stock market assets denominated in several currencies. You protect your investments from currency volatility.

Imagine:

1. You only hold shares denominated in euros.

2. The euro depreciates against the US dollar (this happened in 2022).

3. Your shares lose value...

Conversely, if you also hold assets denominated in US dollars, yen, pounds sterling, Brazilian real, Swiss francs, Australian dollars or Indian rupees, you will offset the depreciation of the euro or any other currency you hold.

Currency diversification helps you reduce investment risk and maximize your chances of success.

C. Asset allocation ratios

Asset allocation ratios are indicators that measure the distribution of your investment between different types of assets, such as shares, ETFs, bonds and cash.

Use this information to determine the ideal percentage of shares, ETFs and cash to include in your portfolio. You can also use these ratios to determine the ideal percentage of sector and geographic diversification for your portfolio.

Take, for example, an investor with a 10-year investment horizon and a high tolerance for risk. He decides to allocate 80% of his portfolio to shares, while keeping 20% in cash.

Asset allocation ratios are tools to help you determine the most appropriate investment strategy for you. However, they are not an exact science and will vary according to many factors, such as market variations and changes in your financial objectives.

3. Portfolios tailored to your age and financial situation!

To adjust your asset allocation strategy to your age and financial situation, it's important to take into account various factors such as your investment horizon, financial objectives, tolerable level of risk and liquidity requirements.

In general, the closer you get to retirement, the wiser it is to increase the proportion of less risky assets such as bonds, ETFs and low-volatility shares.

Conversely, for younger investors with a long-term investment horizon, it makes more sense to invest more in shares and riskier ETFs for higher returns.

Invented by leading investors, these portfolios have already proved their worth to thousands of investors! I still recommend that you take your time to choose the one that suits you best!

A. Jack Bogle's 60/40 portfolio

Who is Jack Bogle?

The 60/40 portfolio was popularized by Jack Bogle, founder of the Vanguard Group. This investment strategy already existed before him.

Bogle simply popularized the idea by making it accessible to everyone, thanks to the creation of index funds!

What does this portfolio consist of?

- Bonds: 60%
- Shares: 40%

For whom is it best suited?

The 60/40 portfolio is considered a popular choice for long-term investors looking to reduce their exposure to market risks while enjoying moderate portfolio growth.

Thus, the typical avatar for this portfolio is a conservative or moderate investor, seeking a balance between capital preservation and long-term growth. This could be someone close to retirement or with a more conservative risk profile.

Benefits

- Dividing your portfolio between shares and bonds helps reduce risk. Bonds tend to be less volatile than shares, offering a degree of portfolio stability in turbulent markets.

- The 60/40 split is easy to set up and manage, making it an attractive option for novice investors or those who prefer a straightforward approach to investing.

- Historically, the 60/40 portfolio has delivered solid, steady returns over the long term, making it suitable for investors looking for a long-term investment.

Disadvantages

- The 60/40 portfolio lacks diversification across asset classes. For example, it does not include asset classes such as real estate, commodities or TIPS Bonds, which offer protection against inflation.

- Because of the high proportion of bonds in the portfolio, long-term returns are more limited. If interest rates rise, bonds offer less attractive returns, limiting the portfolio's gains...

- The 60/40 portfolio is not suitable for all profiles. For example, investors seeking higher yields will prefer other portfolios. Similarly, investors looking for higher income will not find this portfolio suited to their needs.

B. Harry Browne's permanent portfolio

Who is Harry Browne?

Harry Browne was an American economist, author and politician. He was a candidate for President of the United States in 1996 and 2000 for the Libertarian Party. Browne is best known for his long-term investment philosophy based on diversification and risk minimization.

He has written several books on investment, including the well-known :

- "Fail-Safe Investing: Lifelong Financial Security in 30 Minutes".
- "The Permanent Portfolio: Harry Browne's Long-Term Investment Strategy".

Its investment approach is to spread capital evenly across 4 asset classes: shares, bonds, cash and precious metals. This strategy is known as the "Permanent Portfolio".

What does this portfolio consist of?

- Shares: 25%
- Bonds: 25%
- Precious metals (mainly gold): 25%
- Cash (bank + cash): 25%

For whom is it best suited?

This portfolio is generally suitable for investors seeking a more conservative investment approach focused on capital preservation rather than short-term growth.

The most suitable people for this portfolio could be retirees or investors close to retirement who are looking to hedge against market and interest rate risks. Investors who are risk-averse or looking for a more stable investment approach may also find this portfolio suitable.

Benefits

- Diversification: this portfolio is well diversified, comprising 4 different asset classes: bonds, shares, real estate and precious metals. This spread is well suited to counteract risk, since if one asset underperforms, it can be offset by the performance of another.

- Protection against inflation: owning gold helps protect against inflation, as precious metals have historically held their value over time.

- Easy to follow: it's simple to set up and follow, as it doesn't require complex decision-making. Investors allocate their money according to recommended percentages and rebalance their portfolio once a year.

Disadvantages

- Limited return potential: investors seeking to maximize their return may be disappointed by the performance of the Permanent Portfolio. Indeed, it was designed to be a "defensive portfolio", not an "aggressive portfolio".

- High costs: the permanent portfolio is sometimes more expensive than other portfolios, as it includes several different asset classes, which can lead to higher management fees. In addition, holding physical gold entails storage and insurance costs, unless you keep it at home.

- Sensitivity to changes in interest rates: this portfolio is sensitive to changes in interest rates, as it includes a high proportion of bonds. If interest rates rise, the value of bonds falls, which has a negative impact on portfolio performance.

C. David Swensen's portfolio

Who is David Swensen?

David Swensen is a famous American investor and the Chief Investment Officer of the renowned Yale University. He is best known for developing the Yale investment strategy known as the "Swensen Model", widely adopted by many financial institutions.

This strategy focuses on asset diversification, asset allocation and the use of alternative investments. Swensen has also published several books on investing, the best known of which is "Unconventional Success: A Fundamental Approach to Personal Investment".

What does this portfolio consist of?

- U.S. shares: 30%
- International shares (+ Europe): 15%
- Emerging market shares: 5%
- Real estate (REIT): 20%
- Long-term government bonds: 15%
- TIPS Bonds: 15%

A few explanations are in order

What are TIPS Bonds?

TIPS (Treasury Inflation-Protected Securities) are U.S. government bonds designed to protect investors against inflation. TIPS are linked to the Consumer Price Index (CPI), and their values are adjusted in line with inflation.

In practical terms, if inflation rises, so does the nominal value of TIPS, which means that the interest paid by TIPS will also rise. This enables investors to protect their money against inflation.

TIPS are generally considered safe, low-risk investments, as they are issued by the U.S. government. However, as with any investment, there are potential risks, such as the risk of fluctuating interest rates and the risk of higher-than-expected inflation.

What is a REIT?

A REIT (Real Estate Investment Trust) is a company that invests in real estate in the United States.

REITs own, manage and/or finance commercial real estate, such as office buildings, shopping centers, hotels and warehouses, as well as houses, apartments and more. These are listed companies that must comply with certain legal requirements in order to benefit from advantageous tax treatment.

Rental income from real estate assets is generally distributed in the form of dividends to shareholders. REITs offer investors an easy way to invest in real estate without having to buy and manage property directly.

For whom is it best suited?

This type of portfolio is suited to a person with a long-term investment vision and a moderate to high risk tolerance.

In terms of age, this might suit someone between 30 and 50, with a stable profession and regular income.

This person would be willing to take risks to maximize long-term returns, while being aware of the risks.

Benefits

- Diversification: Swensen's portfolio spreads investments across different sectors and asset classes, offering great diversification and reducing overall risk!

- Performance: the portfolio's past performance has been solid, with an average annual return of around 10% for over 2 decades!

- Innovative strategy: Swensen has been an innovator in stock market investing, focusing on less common asset classes such as listed real estate and emerging market shares. This strategy has delivered market-beating returns in the past.

Disadvantages

- High costs: some of the asset classes included in Swensen's portfolio, such as emerging market shares, may require you to pay higher fees when you buy (depending, of course, on the type of broker you use).

- Complexity: Swensen's portfolio can be complex for novice investors, as it uses less common asset classes and more sophisticated investments.

D. The Ivy portfolio

Who developed the Ivy portfolio?

The Ivy Portfolio is an investment strategy developed by the prestigious American universities of Harvard and Yale. This approach is based on in-depth studies of the world of finance, with a particular focus on investment strategies.

Popularized by Mebane Faber, the Ivy portfolio takes its name from the "Ivy League", a group of 8 private universities in the Northeastern United States, among the most prestigious in the world.

The Ivy portfolio is an improvement on the permanent portfolio. Universities have applied this approach to their own funds, investing in the financial markets to give students theoretical and practical training.

What does this portfolio consist of?

- U.S. shares: 20%
- International shares: 20%
- 10-year bonds: 20%
- Commodities : 20
- Real estate (REIT): 20%

For whom is it best suited?

It is suitable for anyone between the ages of 40 and 60 who is looking to minimize risk while achieving satisfactory returns!

This person is looking for a simple, easy-to-manage investment strategy. He or she could be an executive, entrepreneur or self-employed person with a certain level of financial comfort, looking to secure his or her financial future.

Benefits

- Diversification: this portfolio is designed to offer complete diversification by investing in different asset classes. This strategy reduces overall portfolio risk while providing exposure to different markets.

- Reduced volatility: designed to be conservative, this portfolio aims to reduce volatility and protect the investor's capital in times of crisis. 10-year bonds are considered safer investments than international shares.

- Long-term performance: The Ivy portfolio has delivered solid long-term performance. It has outperformed many other diversified portfolios while being less volatile!

Disadvantages

- Low equity allocation: The Ivy portfolio has only a 40% allocation to shares, which may limit the portfolio's long-term growth potential.

- Dependence on commodities: the high proportion of commodities in this portfolio makes it vulnerable to fluctuations. With the exception of gold (and even then, this has to be qualified), other commodities are often volatile.

E. Ray Dalio's portfolio

Who is Ray Dalio?

Ray Dalio is an American investor and hedge fund manager. He is best known as the founder of Bridgewater Associates, one of the world's largest hedge funds, which he set up in 1975.

Dalio has also published several books, the best-known of which is "Principles: Life and Work", in which he shares his principles of personal and professional success.

He is considered a pioneer of quantitative analysis and algorithm-based investment strategies for hedge funds.

What does this portfolio consist of?

- U.S. shares: 30%
- International shares: 15%
- Government bonds: 40%
- Commodities: 7.5%
- TIPS Bonds: 7.5%

For whom is it best suited?

Ray Dalio's "All Weather" portfolio. It is often considered the most suitable portfolio for investors seeking optimal diversification with controlled risk.

This portfolio is designed to withstand all economic conditions, hence the name "All Weather". It is particularly well-suited to investors seeking protection against economic and financial crises, while achieving attractive returns over the long term.

However, it should be noted that this portfolio requires some expertise and active management to get the most out of it, so it is more suited to experienced investors than beginners.

Benefits

- Diversification: this portfolio is designed to be resilient to changing economic conditions, making it suitable for a wide variety of market situations. It is diversified between shares, bonds, commodities and cash.

- Strategic asset allocation: designed to strategically allocate assets according to their performance in different economic environments, rather than focusing solely on short-term performance!

- Inflation protection: TIPS Bonds provide this protection.

- Stable performance: this portfolio aims to generate stable performance over time, which is attractive to investors seeking to avoid short-term fluctuations.

Disadvantages

- Lower performance than some portfolios: this portfolio may not generate returns as high as some portfolios with high equity exposure, during bull markets.

- Complexity: this portfolio can be complex to set up, requiring in-depth knowledge of the financial markets. In addition, it can be difficult to maintain asset allocation over the long term, which may require more frequent rebalancing.

Chapter 7:

How to manage your portfolio like a pro

1. Active or passive portfolio management?

A. A personal decision

Whether to manage your portfolio actively or passively is a personal decision that depends on your time, knowledge and objectives.

The active style involves constant analysis of financial markets and companies to make buy and sell decisions on a regular basis. This management style requires a significant commitment in terms of time and knowledge, but can potentially offer superior gains.

The passive style simply involves buying and holding a portfolio over a long period. This strategy is simpler, requires less time and effort, but offers more modest gains.

B. My advice

I prefer the 100% passive approach to managing my brokerage account.

Less time and effort

By opting for a passive approach, you don't need to devote as much time and effort to managing your portfolio.

You don't need to track the performance of every stock on a daily basis, or make frequent adjustments in response to market fluctuations. You can concentrate on earning more money in your job or in your own business, which you can then invest in your brokerage account!

Reduced costs

The passive approach also minimizes the costs associated with managing your portfolio. ETFs, a popular option for a passive approach, generally have very low management fees compared to actively managed funds.

Superior performance

A Morningstar study entitled "SPIVA Scorecard" and an annual "S&P Dow Jones Indices SPIVA Europe Scorecard" have shown that most actively managed funds fail to beat index returns over the long term! Which means you can potentially achieve superior results, by opting for a passive approach.

→ One study even proved that the biggest performances recorded in stock market portfolios were achieved, by people who forgot they had a stock market portfolio or by people who had died!

Reduced stress

Finally, passive management helps reduce investment stress by minimizing decision-making and market fluctuations. You can focus on your long-term strategy, rather than short-term market fluctuations!

2. How many assets should I put in my portfolio?

A. There is no perfect number!

Some investors have portfolios with 5 assets, while others may have 35 or more!

I recommend having between 10 and 20 lines in your portfolio when you start out. It doesn't matter whether it's stocks, ETFs, bonds or all 3. This gives you adequate diversification, while keeping portfolio management simple.

However, you need to understand that having too many assets can make managing your portfolio complex and difficult to follow, which can lead to mistakes in your investment decisions... Conversely, if you only have 3 assets, you're not diversified enough and you're taking unnecessary risks.

B. Attention

These portfolio examples are general models!

The ideal allocation depends on many personal factors, such as age, financial goals and ability to bear risk. You need to understand your own financial priorities. You also need to take the time to re-evaluate them regularly to ensure that your strategy is still aligned with your objectives.

→ Never forget this: there's no such thing as a perfect portfolio.

Everyone has different financial goals, ages and risk tolerances. What is considered a good portfolio for one person, is not for another.

Basically, there's no point in foolishly copying a portfolio just because a friend uses it or a financial guru advises it. You're not those people, you're unique!

3. Monitor and adjust your portfolio

A. Monitoring your performance

How many times a year should I check my portfolio?

There is no "mandatory" or "perfect" frequency for monitoring a portfolio. In general, I advise you to monitor the performance of your portfolio 1 to 3 times a year, to ensure that your portfolio is still aligned with your objectives.

Many investors monitor their portfolios every day or several times a day...

This kind of "compulsive behavior" risks making you make impulsive decisions based on your emotions, rather than on factual data!

Too frequent monitoring can also cause you to lose sight of your objective, which is counterproductive for you. What's more, you'll be wasting time looking at your portfolio's performance for nothing: that's time lost for other activities!

That's why I recommend limiting your monitoring to 1-3 times a year, so that you can focus on long-term strategy and minimize the impact of emotions on your investment decisions.

Sites and applications to help you

- Yahoo Finance: this site offers information on stock markets, currencies, commodities and stock indices from around the world.

- Google Finance: this site provides data on stock markets, currencies and stock indices from around the world. I prefer it more and more to Yahoo Finance, as I find the information better presented.

- Investing.com: this site offers real-time information on stock markets. It also allows you to create alerts for price changes and track the performance of your portfolio. Honestly, this is the site I use the most before Google finance. I find it clear, easy to use and it's the site I use to get all the ratios. It's thanks to this site that I select all the stocks I buy in my brokerage account.

- TradingView: this site lets you analyze charts of stocks, ETFs and other financial instruments, as well as track market trends and technical indicators.

- Bloomberg: this site provides financial news, real-time market data, analysis and expert commentary. Bloomberg is a world leader in financial data. It's a site you should use in the same way as Investing.com and Google finance. Personally, these are the sites I find most relevant!

- Moning.co: this is a site I'm currently using, created by a French team. I find their interface really interesting. However, you have to pay to obtain certain information that you'll find more difficult to find, on Investing.com, of course, but for free...

Note that this list is not exhaustive, and that it is always advisable to do further research to find the tool that best suits your needs and objectives.

→ Don't forget to check out the "Source" section at the end of the book, which includes all the websites I mention in this book.

B. Adjust according to your objectives and risk tolerance

Asset reallocation

When it comes to making adjustments, I recommend that you do so once a year. In stock market jargon, this is called "asset reallocation".

Asset reallocation involves adjusting the allocation of different asset classes in your portfolio.

This may involve adjusting the proportion of shares, ETFs, bonds, cash and other assets to suit your needs.

To reallocate your assets, follow these steps:

- Review the performance of your assets individually to ensure that your portfolio remains aligned with your financial objectives.
- Determine whether your objectives and risk tolerance have changed.
- Calculate your ideal asset allocation based on your financial goals and risk tolerance.
- Sell assets that have underperformed your financial objectives.
- If necessary, purchase additional assets to achieve the ideal allocation.
- Save your portfolio adjustments. The Moning.co application (paid version) does this automatically, which is a significant time-saver. Of course, it's not the only one with this feature.

Important

You should always carry out your reallocations thoughtfully and without getting carried away by your emotions! It's also important to remember that reallocation is only one element of a long-term investment strategy.

I haven't made any asset reallocations for over 2 years on my PEA, because it wasn't necessary.

As I write these lines, my PEA is showing a performance of +20% (as you can see in the image below, see the 2 red rectangles)! I'm not going to spend my time and energy modifying a strategy that's already working!

Whether it's a PEA or a brokerage account, the principle remains the same!

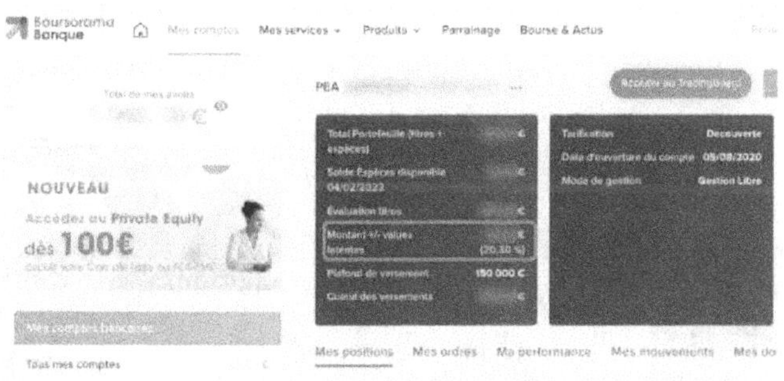

4. Take market opportunities into account

A. Find promising companies

The key to successful investing is to make sure you're investing in the right companies and sectors.

Do your own research to determine whether a company or sector is a good choice for your portfolio. Don't forget to refer to what we've seen in Chapters 4 and 5, to find promising companies in growth sectors.

B. Implement a flexible investment strategy

Be flexible in your investment strategy. Technological developments and changes in economic sectors can open up new opportunities. Don't get stuck in the past, as you could miss out on incredible opportunities.

How many investors missed the opportunity to make a lot of money with the Internet boom in the years 2000-2010, simply because they didn't see the enormous potential of this sector?

→ Be careful not to "jump at every opportunity" that comes your way.

It's always wise to remain vigilant and not get carried away by the first sign of opportunity.

Chapter 8:

Managing stock market risks with confidence

---

1. The risks

The world of stock market investing is not a world of Care Bears! I'm not going to lie to you and tell you that there's no risk involved.

You need to understand the different risks involved in investing in the stock market, as this will help you to manage your portfolio better and make more informed decisions to minimize these risks.

With all due respect to readers, understanding these risks can be challenging, even for the most seasoned investors. It's not about being naive or uninformed, but rather about gaining familiarity with the topic.

That's why I recommend that beginners learn gradually and take the time to understand the different risks, so that they can assess opportunities in an informed and conscious way.

A. Market risks

In this world, there's risk in everything you do, and investing in the stock market is no exception!

You need to understand that financial markets are volatile and that the value of your portfolio fluctuates according to economic, political and even climatic conditions.

When you invest in the stock market, you take on market risk. This means that the value of your investments can fluctuate according to the state of the global economy and the performance of individual companies.

As a long-term investor, it's important not to panic when stocks or ETFs fluctuate. In fact, it's an opportunity to buy stocks or ETFs at a discount, as they'll probably go up again over the long term!

As always, the key to reducing market risk is not to be overly exposed to a single sector, company or market. Diversification is your best friend!

Invest in a variety of companies at different stages of their business cycle and in different sectors to reduce market risk.

Ultimately, it's up to you to decide how much risk you're willing to take.

Don't forget :

- *"The higher the risk, the greater the potential reward!"*

But...

- *"The higher the risk, the higher the risk!"*

So keep this in mind to make informed investment decisions.

B. Risk of capital loss

A risk inherent to all investors

This risk is inherent in any investment: you can lose money if the assets you've purchased don't perform as expected.

It's important not to panic if you encounter this type of situation. In fact, it's an opportunity to learn and grow as an investor.

Investing for the long term helps minimize the risk of capital loss. By investing over a longer period, you give your portfolio time to recover from market volatility, and realize long-term gains.

Even the greatest make mistakes!

Even the biggest investors are suffering losses.

During a recession in the 90s, Warren Buffett lost around 50% of his stock portfolio!

However, he continued to invest for the long term. Just because you're losing money now doesn't mean you're a bad investor!

In 2020, Warren Buffett (him again) declared that he had made a mistake. In April, he and his company Berkshire Hathaway had sold their entire 10% stake in the 4 major US airlines: American Airlines, Delta Air Lines, Southwest Airlines and United Airlines.

Here's what he had to say: "It turns out I was wrong".

C. Risk of company default

When a company is no longer able to repay its debts or continue as a going concern, it is said to be in default. Unfortunately, this can result in a loss for the investors who have put money into the company.

You can minimize this risk by choosing financially sound companies and diversifying your portfolio. That's why I've stressed in previous chapters (particularly in chapter 4) the importance of researching companies before including them in your portfolio!

In short, the risk of corporate default is a risk that every investor must understand and be prepared to manage.

D. Liquidity risks

Saying goodbye to liquidity...

As an investor, it's crucial to be aware of liquidity risks. Liquidity pertains to the ease with which an asset can be sold swiftly without incurring a substantial loss in its value.

Illiquid mutual funds, physical real estate, art or wine are difficult investments to sell quickly when needed.

Illiquid mutual funds, physical real estate, art or wine are difficult investments to sell quickly when needed.

The stock market has the significant advantage of being one of the most liquid investments.

On the other hand, some stocks and ETFs are not very liquid. Their low trading volume makes it more difficult to sell them quickly when needed.

For example, some small-cap stocks have limited trading volumes, making them less liquid. Similarly, some ETFs specializing in niche sectors or emerging markets may be illiquid.

More than $500 million

That's why, in my investment criteria, I told you to invest in companies with a market capitalization of $500 million and ETFs with assets under management of over $100 million!

By following these rules, you considerably increase your chances of being able to resell your assets easily.

In fact, there will always be a sufficient number of potential buyers to enable you to sell quickly without running into liquidity problems.

E. Political and geopolitical risks

In this uncertain world, political and geopolitical risks have a significant impact on stock market investments.

For example, a war or a change of government can have an impact on businesses and therefore on your investments.

When you invest in the stock market, you have to take into account the risk in the world we live in.

You need to be aware of world events that may have an impact on your investments.

Finally, I'd like to remind you that there's no such thing as a risk-free investment!

2. Managing the risks of stock market investing

A. The importance of diversification

In the stock market, diversification is the key to managing risk. By diversifying your portfolio, you spread your capital over several stocks/ETFs, business sectors and countries.

This way, if a company or sector falls on hard times, you're not entirely exposed to that risk, as you have other assets to offset losses.

No one has a crystal ball to predict the future of the economy or companies. That's why diversification is a basic and essential technique for managing the risks associated with stock market investing.

B. Why it's so important!

I couldn't manage my stress...

I still remember the times when I couldn't manage the stress of investing in my brokerage account. At the start of my career, I had invested everything in just 2 stocks.

I was often anxious, because I knew that if one of these 2 stocks fell significantly, it would have a considerable impact on my portfolio. I was stressed by every movement in stock prices and often woke up at night to check the performance of my shares.

It was a difficult time for me, because I was constantly stressed at the thought of losing all my money.

It was then that I realized the importance of diversifying my portfolio. I started looking at new sectors and investing in different stocks to spread my risk. By taking these steps, I was finally able to reduce my stress.

Investing shouldn't be a source of stress

I'd like to remind you that investment is there to create wealth for you. On the contrary, it's there to reassure you and give you peace of mind.

When I bet everything on 2 stocks, I quickly realized that it was a mistake. All my savings were concentrated in these stocks. I realized that I was jeopardizing my financial security by not diversifying my portfolio.

That's why I encourage you not to make the same mistake I did. You can do it by investing in stocks from different industries, by buying ETFs or by doing both!

Never forget that investing is a game of patience. Don't be distracted by short-term fluctuations, and stay focused on your long-term strategy.

Wealth isn't created overnight, but it accumulates over time if you remain patient and disciplined! As the saying goes: "Rome wasn't built in a day"!

Chapter 9:

Find the right

broker for you

---

1. Take the time to make the right choice

A. What to consider

To make the best choice of broker for your brokerage account, it's important to consider several criteria.

Precision

You'll often see the word "broker" pop up when you're doing your research. It simply means "broker" in English.

Here are a few things to consider:

- Brokerage fees: it's important to compare the fees charged by different brokers in order to choose the one that offers the best value for money.
- Tools: check out the tools provided by the broker to carry out your trades (this simply means your buy and sell orders). Online platforms, mobile applications and analysis tools must meet your needs!

- Quality of customer support: make sure the broker has reliable customer support available to answer all your questions.

- The broker's reputation and experience: choose a well-established broker with solid experience in the investment field.

- Available investment options: make sure the broker offers the investment options you want. For example, some brokers do not offer certain ETFs or stocks.

B. Different types of broker

Online brokers

Online brokers are becoming increasingly popular with stock market investors, due to their affordability and accessibility. They allow investors to manage their accounts online and have access to real-time monitoring tools. There are many online brokers offering brokerages accounts.

Here are some of the most popular and serious brokers:

- Interactive Broker: the broker for pros! Honestly, it's the Rolls-Royce of brokers!
- De Giro
- eToro (I absolutely do not recommend it, as it has the highest fees I've ever seen!)
- Trade Republic

Traditional brokers

I absolutely do not recommend traditional brokers, and even less so banks. Traditional brokers are not adapted to modern use and their commissions literally eat into your returns!

The only ones who'll get rich are them, not you!

I know that some people feel more comfortable trusting a banker, but I can assure you that this is a very bad idea. Even if you have a cordial relationship with him, don't forget that you're investing to make yourself rich, not to make him rich through the commissions you're going to give him...

Mind you, I'm not saying that online brokers don't charge commission. However, their commissions are much fairer and much more affordable!

2. Choosing the right broker

A. Assess your needs

Before choosing a broker, it's important to consider your investment needs. You need to assess your level of investment knowledge and experience, as well as your risk tolerance.

Based on these criteria, you'll be able to determine whether you need a broker who offers you personalized support, or whether you'd prefer to opt for an online platform that lets you manage your investments yourself. Take the time to consider your needs carefully, so you can make the best choice of broker.

B. Research brokers' rates and commissions

In the stock market, a small difference in costs means a big difference in gains over the long term. That's why I recommend that you compare the fees and commissions of different brokers.

Take the time to research how much each transaction will cost you. Find out about account maintenance fees, inactivity fees and closing fees. Not all brokers charge these fees, but some still do...

You're investing to maximize your earnings, so don't forget to take costs into account when making your choice of broker. Ultimately, you want to use a broker that offers a good balance between affordable rates and a solid platform to help you achieve your financial goals!

C. Check fund security and regulations

Investing your money is never a decision to be taken lightly!

It is therefore essential to ensure that the broker you choose is regulated and that your funds are safe.

Regulatory bodies

In the US, the SEC (Securities and Exchange Commission) is the financial markets regulator. It publishes a blacklist of unauthorized brokers in the US. If the broker you've chosen appears on this list, it means that he or she does not comply with security and investor protection standards!

Here is a list of the regulatory authorities for financial markets in various countries:

- UK: Financial Conduct Authority (FCA)
- Australia: Australian Securities and Investments Commission (ASIC)
- Canada : Autorité des marchés financiers (AMF)

Note: Names and responsibilities of authorities may vary from country to country.

Check current and past customer reviews of the broker you've chosen, to get an idea of the quality of their service and overall experience. For this, I highly recommend the Trustpilot site, as the reviews can hardly be faked.

You risk almost nothing with the following two brokers:

- Interactive Broker
- De Giro

In fact, they are managed by major financial bodies and have undergone all the necessary controls.

D. Evaluate the tools and features available

As an investor, you need a broker who offers you the tools and functionality you need to make the best investment decisions. Make sure the broker you choose offers a reliable, easy-to-use platform, as well as research and analysis tools to help you make informed decisions.

For example, Trading 212 provides its customers with advanced tools, such as real-time charts, ratios and technical analysis, enabling you to make informed decisions.

In addition, you need to ensure that your broker offers a high level of security to protect your funds and financial information. Look for brokers who use state-of-the-art security protocols and encryption systems to protect your information.

Finally, think about the overall user experience. You want a broker that's easy to use, with a user-friendly interface and quality customer support to answer all your questions.

E. Feedback

I'd like to share my feedback with you. To be totally honest and transparent with you, I currently use 2 brokers:

- Trade Republic
- Trading 212

Why do I use 2?

I use 2 of them to take advantage of the best features offered by these 2 brokers and I also do it to minimize my risks.

Indeed, these 2 platforms are much more recent and therefore less solid than platforms such as Interactive Brokers or De Giro. In fact, as I write these lines, I'm in the process of opening an account with Interactive Brokers!

Trade Republic

I find that Trade Republic's customer service is still not good enough. For a broker with so many customers, the service is too slow.

On the other hand, their website and app are easy to use.

One of the best things about this platform is its simplicity when you're just starting out. The platform gets straight to the point, and there's no heap of information to overwhelm you as soon as you open it.

What I also like about Trade Republic is that they offer many more financial products and countries to invest in than the Trading 212 platform.

Trading 212

I find the platform much more advanced than Trade Republic. However, I don't find them transparent enough when it comes to fees.

What I don't like about this platform is that the shares are not held in your name, but via contracts known as CFDs.

Basically, CFDs (the acronym stands for "contract for difference") are financial products that enable you to bet on the rise or fall of an "underlying asset" **without ever owning it.**

My little brother has a brokerage account at Interactive Brokers, so I can confirm that their customer service is top-notch, as is the user experience.

However, the site isn't necessarily user-friendly for beginners.

Conversely, Trade Republic or T212 have platforms that are much more suitable for beginners. However, the problem with these 2 platforms lies in the fact that they are much younger and not as "tried and tested" as older brokers such as Interactive Brokers or De Giro.

Chapter 10:

Legal tricks to save taxes

1. The different taxes

A. Why reduce your taxes?

When it comes to personal finance, it's important to maximize profits and minimize expenses. That's where tax reduction comes in.

The more you can reduce your taxes, the more money you have to invest in other opportunities that can help you reach your financial goals faster. Ultimately, it's a way of ensuring you have more control over your money and making it work for you.

B. Dividend tax

Dividends are the income generated by a company's shares. In most countries, dividends are subject to income tax, but tax rates vary from country to country.

For example, in France, dividends are subject to a single flat-rate withholding tax (PFU) of 30%, while in Belgium they are subject to a progressive rate of up to 30%...

C. *Capital gains tax*

Capital gains are the gains realized on the sale of a stock market asset. Stock market investors with a brokerage account are subject to capital gains tax, but tax rules vary from country to country.

In the US, for example, capital gains tax rates vary based on the duration the asset was held; short-term capital gains are taxed as ordinary income, while long-term capital gains benefit from preferential rates which can range from 0% to 20% or more, depending on the individual's income. In Canada, 50% of capital gains are taxable, and they are included in an individual's income and taxed at their marginal tax rate.

D. Important!

At the risk of repeating myself, tax systems vary considerably from country to country. They are totally different whether you live in the US, the UK, Australia, or Canada!

The information provided in this section is for information purposes only and should not be construed as tax advice. It is essential to consult a tax expert or financial advisor for advice tailored to your personal situation.

2. How can I legally optimize my taxes?

A. Accumulating ETFs

Buying capitalisation ETFs is an interesting way of minimizing taxes on dividends, especially if you are resident in France for tax purposes.

Unlike distributing ETFs, accumulating ETF ETFs do not pay dividends to investors, as they reinvest dividends directly in the ETF.

As a result, investors are not taxed on the dividends distributed, because there are none!

Gains generated by accumulating ETFs are, however, subject to capital gains tax as soon as you sell them.

By choosing accumulating ETFs, gains are not distributed, but reinvested to generate further gains. This may not seem important to you, but over the medium and long term, it makes a big difference thanks to the effect of compound interest!

By deferring taxation of gains until sale, you reduce your tax burden. This strategy is ideal for long-term investors who want to maximize their gains and stay in France.

→ Basically, it's better to be taxed at 30% on $100 000 than on $10 000 even if it's still the same tax bracket, because at the end you'll be left with more than you started with!

B. Using losses to reduce taxes

Important

You need to understand the difference between :

- real added value
- an unrealized capital gain

and...

- a real capital loss
- an unrealized capital loss

When you buy a financial asset, such as a share, its price can go up or down. If the price rises and you sell the share, you realize a real capital gain, i.e. you make money. On the other hand, if the price falls and you sell the share, you realize a real capital loss, i.e. you lose money.

On the other hand, if you have not sold your financial asset, the change in its value is said to be latent. For example, if you bought a share at $100 and its price is now $120, you have an unrealised gain of $20. However, this gain will only be realized if you sell the share. The same is true for an unrealized capital loss: as long as you haven't sold the financial asset, the loss is only on paper!

Taxation is not based on unrealized capital gains and losses!

Taxation is based on the actual capital gains realized on the sale of a financial asset (shares, ETFs, etc.)!

If an investor realizes an unrealized capital gain on a financial asset, he will not be taxed. Taxation only arises when the investor sells the financial asset with a capital gain. In addition, if an investor realizes an actual capital loss, he or she can use this loss to reduce tax on gains realized on actual capital gains.

C. My last piece of advice

I hope all this tax jargon hasn't given you too much of a headache!

It was essential for me to provide you with the most relevant information, so that you don't get caught out by the tax complexities...

If you ever have any unanswered questions, I strongly recommend that you consult a tax expert or ask your broker for advice! After all, sometimes it's better to waste a little time or money consulting specialists, than to make rash choices that will cost you more in the long run...

What's more, we mustn't forget that laws evolve. What was true yesterday may no longer be true today!

Give your honest opinion!

Your suggestions and criticisms are invaluable.

They make every reading experience even more satisfying!

Thank you very much for reading my book.

I wish you all the success you deserve!

Conclusion

Are you still intimidated by the idea of investing in the stock market? With all the information and technical terms, it can seem daunting.

If so, the real question you should be asking is:

"Why would I pass up an opportunity to grow my wealth and build a solid financial future?"

In this book, I've given you all the keys to understanding stock market investing with the brokerage account. You've learned about the different investment strategies and how they'll help you achieve your financial goals. Don't let the fear of the unknown paralyze you - it's time to take control of your financial future and change your situation!

By not investing in the financial markets, people lose the chance to grow their wealth and realize their dreams. Don't let inflation reduce the value of your money over time...

Discover the best strategies to optimize your investments and the mistakes to avoid. With my clear and educational approach, my books are suitable for everyone, whether you're a beginner or an experienced investor.

Investing will hold no secrets for you, and you'll be able to build a strong portfolio for your financial future.

Don't wait, get my books now to help you achieve your goals!

I sincerely thank you for reading my book and wish you all the success you deserve!

Gabriel Massias

Sources

Books

- Hagstrom, R. G. (2013). *The Warren Buffett Way*. Wiley.
- Graham, B., & Zweig, J. (2023). *The Intelligent Investor Rev Ed: The Definitive Book on Value Investing*. Generic.
- Kabbaj, T., & Joulié, J. J. (2011). *Psychologie des grands traders*. Eyrolles.
- Lynch, P. (1999). *What if you knew enough to win in the stock market*. VALOR.
- Lynch, P., & Rothchild, J. (2012). *Beating the Street*. Simon & Schuster.
- Fisher, P. A. (2000). *Ordinary shares and extraordinary profits*. Valor.
- Horny, G. (2022). *Je me mets à la bourse pour les Nuls*. FIRST.

Sites

Important note

The sites mentioned are provided for information purposes only and in no way constitute investment advice. It is important to note that these links are not affiliation links and do not generate any remuneration for the author or publisher.

Official regulatory bodies :

- **United States**: Official website of the Securities and Exchange Commission (SEC) : www.sec.gov
- **United Kingdom**: Financial Conduct Authority (FCA) Official website of the FCA: www.fca.org.uk
- **Australia**: Australian Securities and Investments Commission (ASIC) Official website of the ASIC: www.asic.gov.au
- **Canada**: Official website of Canadian Securities Administrators (CSA): www.securities-administrators.ca

Brokers :

- Interactive Brokers: https://www.interactivebrokers.ie/en/home.php

- Degiro: www.degiro.com
- Trade Republic: www.traderepublic.com
- Trading 212: www.trading212.com

Other sites :

- Google Finance: www.google.com/finance/?hl=fr
- Yahoo Finance : https://fr.finance.yahoo.com/
- S&P Global Ratings: www.spglobal.com/ratings/en/index
- Motley Fool: www.fool.com/
- Seeking Alpha : https://seekingalpha.com/
- Forbes Investing: www.forbes.com/investing/
- Investing.com: www.investing.com
- Bloomberg: www.bloomberg.com/markets
- Morning Star: www.morningstar.fr/fr/
- Exchange zone: www.zonebourse.com

- Trustpilot: https://fr.trustpilot.com/

Images

- www.freepik.com
- www.google.com/finance

www.ingramcontent.com/pod-product-compliance
Lightning Source LLC
LaVergne TN
LVHW022054200926
848481LV00003B/907
* 9 7 9 8 2 3 1 8 6 8 2 8 5 *